The Crafts of Williamsburg

THE WORLD OF WILLIAMSBURG

The Crafts
of Williamsburg

Text by James S. Wamsley
Photographs by N. Jane Iseley and Daniel L. Spangler

The Colonial Williamsburg Foundation
Williamsburg, Virginia

Library of Congress Cataloging in Publication Data

Wamsley, James S.
The Crafts of Williamsburg.

(The World of Williamsburg)
1. Handicraft — Virginia — Williamsburg.
2. Williamsburg (Va.) — Social life and customs.
I. Title. II. Series.
TT24. V8W35   670   82-1305
ISBN 0-87935-064-4   AACR2
ISBN 0-87935-065-2 (pbk.)

This book was designed by Vernon Wooten

PRINTED IN THE UNITED STATES OF AMERICA

The following craftsmen and women were serving as masters, journeymen and women, and apprentices at Colonial Williamsburg as of June 1, 1982. **Apothecary:** William Cabell, supervisor; **Bakery:** Dennis Cotner, supervisor; **Blacksmith:** Peter Ross, journeyman, supervisor, David Burcham, journeyman, supervisor, Robert Rowe, Richard Guthrie, Ed Smith, apprentices; **Bootmaker:** Eugene Brown, supervisor, Robert Shaffer, LaMont Carter, journeymen; **Cabinetmaker:** Wright Horne, master, David Salisbury, Kelley Blanton, Kaare Loftheim, apprentices; **Coach and Livestock:** Victor Shone, manager, Joe Jones, assistant manager; **Cooper:** George Pettengell, master, James Pettengell, Lew LeCompte, journeymen, Kerry Shackelford, apprentice; **Domestic Crafts:** Mary Stebbins, manager, Roy Black, supervisor, Bernetta Wake, supervisor; **Foundry:** Sven Dan Berg, Jr., master, George Hassell, Chris Dunham, journeymen; **Gunsmith:** Gary Brumfield, master, Jon Laubach, journeyman, George Suiter, apprentice; **Harnessmaker:** Irvin Diehl, journeyman, supervisor; **Housewright:** Roy Underhill, master, Mark Berninghausen, Bill Weldon, apprentices; **Milliner:** Eleanor Cabell, supervisor; **Musical Instrument Maker:** George Wilson, master, Marcus Hansen, journeyman; **Needlework:** Elizabeth Ackert, needleworker; **Printing Office Complex:** Sandra Yoder, journeywoman, manager, Willie Parker, journeyman, supervisor-press room, Dale Dippre, Mark Howell, Robert Lyon, apprentices; **Silversmith:** James Curtis, journeyman, manager, George Cloyed, apprentice, Judy Luther, apprentice engraving; **Wheelwright:** Dan Stebbins, journeyman, supervisor, Jim Fuller, apprentice; **Wigmaker:** Gail Cauthorne, supervisor; **Windmill:** Cornelius Black, supervisor.

Introduction

fig. 2.

Eighteenth-century craftsmen created a wide variety of products that were essential to everyday life. It took time, perseverance, skill, and determination to supply the needs of a pre-industrial society in which nearly everything had to be produced manually. Skilled hands and nimble fingers milled the corn, baked the bread, sewed the shoes and the harness and the clothes, hammered the tools, and fashioned some of the luxury goods that colonial Virginians needed. Although many items were imported from England, the demand for merchandise of all kinds exceeded the ability of London merchants to supply it, so some products were made locally. Williamsburg's artisans knew full well that their livelihood depended on their ability to produce well-made wares that would appeal to their clientele. From the simplest to the most complex, most of the objects that they created reflected the pride of craftsmanship common to the artisans of the eighteenth century.

In Williamsburg, artisans represented the largest single occupational group, totaling over 40 percent in 1775. More than sixty different crafts — depending on certain niceties of definition — were practiced in Virginia's colonial capital.

The backgrounds of the eighteenth-century craftsmen of Williamsburg were as diverse as the trades they plied. Research indicates that many came as immigrant artisans from Europe, sometimes as indentured servants in return for payment of their passage. Orphaned or unsupported children learned skills under the guardianship of a master of a trade. Some craftsmen moved to Virginia from other colonies. Still another source was the large group of slaves. Records show that blacks worked in several trades, particularly in carpentry, shoemaking, coopering, and blacksmithing.

The apprentice system provided the necessary training and was the way for future craftsmen to acquire their skills. Ideally, a young man was "bound out" at age fourteen so that when he attained journeyman status after a seven-year indenture, he would be able to pursue a trade on his own. The end of his apprenticeship would thus coincide with his coming of age. In practice, a young man could enter into an apprentice agreement at almost any age, and he served a term of years that varied from as few as three to as many as eight.

In addition to being instructed in the "art and mystery" or "trade and mystery" of his master's craft, the apprentice was usually taught to read and write and perhaps to cipher as well. The master also commonly provided "meat, drink, cloaths, washing and lodging" to the young charge, who in turn was obliged to serve the master faithfully, keep his secrets, eschew matrimony, and avoid boisterous pastimes. Females generally were restricted to domestic work, but slaves and free blacks alike served apprenticeships in nearly every trade.

When the apprentice completed his term of indenture, he usually received a suit of clothes, a set of tools — "as many tools as shall be thought sufficient to build a clapboard house" in one case — and perhaps a start-up stake of cash. Now he was a journeyman, free to go anywhere and work at his trade. The term master applied only to the owner of a shop, a state to which the fledgling journeyman undoubtedly aspired.

At Colonial Williamsburg today, more than one hundred men and women ply over thirty trades much like the kinds that flourished here in the years before the American Revolution. Efforts to establish and carry forward the crafts program have been aided by extensive and on-going research. Historians have examined letters, wills, inventories, court records, account books, and the pages of the *Virginia Gazette* to gather information about occupations, job sites, furnishings, equipment, and clothing. Archaeologists have uncovered shop foundations and artifacts that are important clues to the character of production. Architectural research supplied the information essential for the physical restoration or rebuilding of the structures.

An invaluable source of information about colonial crafts is Denis Diderot's thirty-three-volume *Encyclopédie*, published in the mid-eighteenth century. The explanatory text and extraordinarily detailed plates show how work was performed, how tools were used and what they looked like, and how craft shops were arranged and furnished.

Most Williamsburg craftsmen participate in a formal apprentice training program that culminates in the coveted title of "journeyman with all the rights, honors and privileges pertaining thereto." Thus the diffident young apprentice learns by practicing and refining his trade and in time becomes a confident journeyman and perhaps even a highly proficient master craftsman.

Just as in colonial days, many of the products created by Colonial Williamsburg's talented artisans are used where appropriate or are offered for sale to the general public. Like their eighteenth-century prototypes, each article has been carefully hand-fashioned using time-honored tools and methods. Each bears the stamp of the style and temperament of the skilled craftsman or woman who made it.

The engravings that appear on the endsheets and throughout the book are from Denis Diderot, *Encyclopédie ou Dictionnaire Raisonné des Sciences, des Arts et des Métiers.*

Printing Complex

They called it the bar, and pulling it was not for the weak or the small because a minimum weight of 160 pounds was reckoned necessary for the man at the bar. Once every 15 seconds, 240 times per hour, perhaps for 14 hours a day, the puller heaved his arms and back against the bar, creating pressure of 200 pounds per square inch on a fresh sheet of paper.

The Williamsburg shop of William Parks was a communications and graphic arts center for the colony. It combined the functions of a newspaper printing office, book bindery, stationery store, and post office as well as producing books, controversial political tracts, and the hundreds of forms needed by an increasingly literate society.

To master the press — still essentially as Gutenberg had designed it — required a great deal more than a strong back. The printer needed high degrees of literacy and dexterity merely to set type. He kept his characters in sectioned wooden cases, rapidly plucking out the tiny metal slabs as he built each word, then sentence, then paragraph in his hand-held stick. As the composition grew, he transferred it to a galley

The compositor deftly plucks one tiny character at a time from his compartmented trays, or cases, of type, building words and sentences in his composing stick. Capital letters are always kept in the upper case.

The type is transferred from the composition stick to a wooden tray called a galley. Then the compositor slides the type, tied with string, onto a flat marble stone where an entire page will be composed.

The printer locks up his page of type in an iron frame called a chase, hammering in hardwood blocks and wedges so tightly that the finished page may be picked up and carried to the press without falling to pieces.

The puller gives a strong, smooth yank on the press's bar, screwing the platen down and forcing the paper onto the inked type below.

tray and then to a stone imposing table, where it was locked up in an iron frame called a chase. For a mid-eighteenth-century newspaper like the *Virginia Gazette* of Williamsburg, one page of typesetting required about 25 hours. Woe betide the unlucky apprentice who dropped and "pied" the job!

Safely on the press bed, each page of type was shimmed and adjusted in the make-ready stage to produce as uniform an impression as possible. Forms for two newspaper pages were made ready on the press, although only one page at a time could be printed. Thus printers called it a two-pull press.

The puller was half a press team. The other half was the beater, whose main job was to spread ink uniformly across the type for each fresh impression. He wielded a pair of ink balls, leather-covered pads with wooden handles with which he transferred the sticky ink from a marble slab, vigorously pounding the type, knowing by feel when he had inked enough.

Type was forever wearing out, and the printer needed a regular, reliable source of supply. Some bought new characters regularly from such famed type founders as England's William Cas-

lon. Type was cast by pouring a molten alloy of lead, tin, and antimony into a mold, or matrix, for each character. Making the molds was virtually a craft in itself; so, too was cutting the reusable wood-block illustrations and ornaments that dressed up a page.

Paper supply was another problem. Williamsburg's Parks tried to solve it around 1743 by starting his own paper mill. Whatever the source, the paper of the day, handmade from linen rags, was uneven in texture. To gain a decent impres-

Working at top speed, the puller and the beater may make one impression every 15 seconds, or 240 times per hour.

Sticky ink made of varnish and lampblack is stirred to a molasses-like consistency on a mixing stone. With leather-covered ink balls the beater inks the type before each impression.

sion, the printer dampened each sheet before laying it on the press.

Becoming a journeyman printer required a long apprenticeship, while reaching the state of master printer was — compared to other trades — very difficult. The master owned the printing shop, which required a far greater capital investment than most trades. He was therefore a man of property, and probably a shrewd businessman as well.

William Parks, Virginia's most noted colonial printer, was all that and more, for he added a bindery known for the quality and variety of its books.

By its routine production of blank record books, almanacs, ledgers, and governmental session laws and codes the bindery provided an

1. Most colonial printers ordered type from England or Holland. The type-founder begins by cutting his own steel punch for each character. He hammers an impression into a piece of copper, which becomes a mold, or matrix.

2. The depth of each matrix character is critical since every piece of type must be precisely the same height. Eighteenth-century typefounders used small, accurate depth gauges like this to measure the "depth of drive" after punching a letter into the matrix.

3. Casting new type begins with a molten blend of lead, tin, and antimony.

4. The printer pours a hot mixture of lead, tin, and antimony into the mold that encloses a single matrix.

5. The matrix is removed from the printer's type mold and a "B" emerges.

A finished printed piece is ready to be removed from the frame and folded.

essential service in early Virginia. At his peak of quality and skill, the binder created both durable, utilitarian bindings and fashionable gold-tooled designs of lasting elegance.

Much of the printer's work was ready for distribution the moment the ink dried, but in the case of books the sheet that came from the press contained at least four pages, arranged so that folding and cutting would place them in sequence. Proper folding, the binder's first task, created signatures of four, eight, twelve, or sixteen pages. The right number of sequential signatures in hand, the binder began stitching them together at his sewing frame.

Strong linen thread looped through the paper folds, binding them to thick vertical cords of hemp stretched in the sewing frame. Those latter crossbands gave the finished book its characteristic ridges across the spine, its toughness, and its easy, flat opening. Stitching done, the binder glued the whole spine together, trimmed off the three unglued sides, and then attached the cover boards. So far, the work was skilled but ultimately unseen. From that point on, the binder's

With the deckle and mold, a screen-like device, a vatman scoops up the soggy pulp that will become a sheet of paper.

In a process called "couching off," the papermaker eases a flat wet mass of rag fiber onto a felt mat. Layered with others, it will be placed in a screw press and squeezed to remove water and compress the mass into a sheet.

To obtain the rags from which eighteenth-century paper was made, printers ran advertisements and made their offices collection points. Most rags were linen, not cotton. Fibers were softened in a series of processes before going to the vat (left) and then the "couching off" stage (center).

A wooden screw press mashes the water from a stack of new paper alternating with felt mats. Felt removed, the paper will be stacked into one hundred-sheet packs and squeezed again.

9

artistry could assert itself. Soft, supple leathers — dyed a rich blue, red, green, or, predominantly, brown — now were drawn onto the boards and were glued on the inside and water-dampened on the outside. The final embellishments were added when the binder heated his wheeled brass tools and applied designs to the leather. Sometimes he applied gold leaf.

For a colorful finishing touch, the eighteenth-century bookbinder occasionally used marbled endpapers that he imported from English craftsmen. One of the most colorful skills related to bookbinding, marbling requires only a small tank containing a mixture of water and syrupy gum tragacanth, plus assorted vivid watercolors.

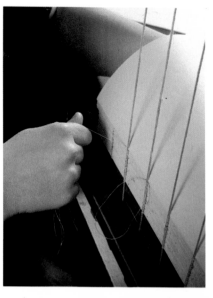

Folded signatures of paper that contain four to sixteen pages are stitched together at the bookbinder's sewing frame, one of the first stages in manufacturing a book.

About to receive its leather binding, a new book clearly displays the exposed spinal crossbands that give hand-bound books their distinctive ridges.

Leather book bindings are dyed in various colors. Brown predominates.

Sheets of gold on a newly bound book await the impression of a corner ornamenting fleuron stamp. The edges of the pages have already been decorated by the marbleizing process.

Once a binding is complete, the craftsman may decorate it with a variety of patterns rolled and stamped in gold leaf. First heated, the binder's tools then impress attractive gilded borders.

Fixed as they fall by a mixture of gum tragacanth, droplets of vivid watercolors are added to the paper marbling tank.

Held fast by the syrup, the colors, shaken in drops onto the tank solution's surface, refuse to blend or spread. Then with a series of combs the craftsman draws abstract, swirling patterns through the colors. Satisfied with the design, he lays a clean sheet of paper on the surface, gently presses it down, and pulls forth a miracle of blues, reds, and yellows.

While marbling was not, apparently, performed in the colonies, the use here of imported marbled paper affirmed the colorful technique as an ingredient of Williamsburg bookbinding. Marbling's demonstration today adds a final exciting touch to the graphic arts crafts reincarnated in William Parks's shop.

With special combs the craftsman creates swirling, abstract patterns of brilliant color.

A sheet of white paper is laid gently on the surface. When it is removed, the marbled design appears on it. After drying, it will be pasted into a book as an endpaper.

Gunsmith

Gunsmithing is a complex and difficult craft and the man who masters it must be blacksmith, machinist, foundryman, woodcarver, and engraver.

There were no graceful long rifles when Virginia's first gunsmith arrived in 1608, only heavy, clumsy muskets with matchlock, wheel lock, and snaphance ignition systems. Repairing such weapons, nearly all imported from England and consigned to militiamen, occupied most gunsmiths of the early colony.

At least a few guns were made in Virginia by the late 1600s, coinciding with the perfection of the lighter, more efficient flintlock system. In the mid-eighteenth century, a distinctive new weapon appeared, both accurate and beautiful. Evolving in the colonies from hunting rifles carried by German immigrants to Pennsylvania, Maryland, and Virginia, the long rifle proved the ideal weapon for America and became the very symbol of the frontiersman.

Today it is a classic antique and a popular reproduction subject, but only a handful of gifted craftsmen can create a long rifle in the authentic way.

The job that takes more than three hundred hours begins at the forge. Bar iron, heated almost white hot, is hammered flat and then is shaped into a crude tube. Around a poker-like mandril and hammered across a shape-setting swage

An American long rifle begins at the forge, where gunsmiths flatten a bar of iron for the barrel skelp.

Guided by the contours of an oddly shaped anvil called the swage block, the hammerman welds the iron skelp around a poker-like mandril to fashion the barrel.

13

Rifling gives the weapon its name and the bullet its spin. To produce it, the gunsmith cuts seven perfectly spaced spiral grooves inside the bore with the aid of this rifling machine.

block, the barrel takes form through hundreds of heatings. Next the smith bores out the new barrel's interior to a straight, smooth tunnel. Then the exterior is smoothed to perfection by hand filing. The top five flats receive an extra polish with emery compound. That done, the bore is rifled with seven spiraling grooves, a process aided by an ingenious machine like a giant corkscrew.

Making the barrel takes six days. To test it, the smith takes the barrel outside, lashes it to an enormous oak board, and by a lighted powder train fires a charge four times the future weapon's normal load.

The barrel is one of gunsmithing's two most difficult single steps. Making the lock is the other. The flintlock system, developed in the early seventeenth century and dominant for more than two hundred years, was the ultimate device for striking sparks. A piece of sharpened flint, locked

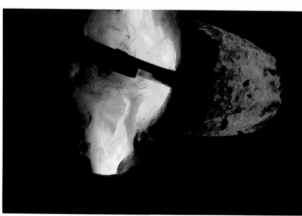

The mastery of some foundry techniques allows the gunsmith to cast his own brass furniture, chiefly the butt plate and trigger guard.

in a small movable vise named the cock (often incorrectly called the hammer), smashes into a spring-loaded projection, the frizzen, pushing it forward and directing a shower of sparks into the thus exposed powder pan. The flash of igniting powder then travels through a tiny hole in the barrel to set off the main charge.

Forging the lockplate from white-hot iron takes only thirty minutes, but filing it to shape is a task that requires many hours. Then all the tiny moving parts are forged and filed in relationship to each other. Each lock requires a mainspring and two smaller springs. For those, the smith needs expensive spring steel, which he must forge to shape, file, polish, heat in boiling lead, and quench in linseed oil.

Two major brass parts, the butt plate and trigger guard, must be cast. The master carefully sets his pattern in wet sand, heats brass to the boiling point, and pours. The rough castings that result are patiently filed.

A curly maple plank, dried at least three years, becomes the stock. Bedding the barrel is critical: scribing, gouging, planing, and fine chiseling ultimately ease the barrel into a solid groove. Fitting the butt plate governs the stock's rear contours. A myriad of small parts must be made and fitted — trigger, forend cap, ramrod thimbles, patchbox, and sideplate. Some metal parts like the patchbox (a container of tallow-greased loading patches) are always engraved. If the rifle is a fancy one, silver ornaments like stars and acorns are made and inlaid, and relief carving graces the wood. Simple or elaborate, the American long rifle is a work of art, a piece of practical sculpture, a useful masterpiece.

1. Metal parts are inlet into the maple stock. Soot from a candle marks their shape.

2. Parts of the lock are forged and then fitted together by hand filing.

6. Heat is applied to nitric acid to darken the stock's finish.

4. - 5. Engraving the patchbox, as in this typical Virginia design, is one of the final steps.

3. The addition of raised carving adds greatly to its beauty.

4.

5.

Cabinetmaker

Of all the vanished masters of eighteenth-century Williamsburg, none left clearer artistic testimony than the cabinetmakers, whose works are compounded of skill, taste, and fashion.

How unfair, then, that their reputations — great in their own time — became obscured during Williamsburg's post-Revolutionary decline. Although many pieces survived, succeeding generations of owners forgot the origins of their assorted tables, presses, chairs, desks, and bookcases. Revived as desirable antiques in recent years, they were misattributed to other colonial centers or to England. The masters of Williamsburg were remembered vaguely as the source of simple furniture for undemanding customers.

But research in the last decade has permanently, and dramatically, dislodged that fiction. Today it is known that Williamsburg cabinetmakers produced superior work for a discriminating, fashion-conscious clientele. Furniture from such men as Peter Scott, Anthony Hay, Benjamin Bucktrout, and Edmund Dickinson was usually ahead of Philadelphia and New England in fashion and was superior in construction.

Wealthy Virginians demanded their furniture in the latest urban English mode, which sometimes meant conservative to the point of austerity. The preference for restraint endured through the periods of George I and II (sometimes erroneously linked with the earlier Queen Anne), rococo

17

The lathe, an ancient power tool, was commonplace in eighteenth-century furniture shops. Some, like this one, were cranked by hand; water or foot power drove others.

The artisan shapes a molding with a molding plane.

Parts are shaped with a plane.

Dovetailing, a basic skill for any journeyman, was a technique used in the construction of drawers.

(Chippendale), and neoclassic. Northern cabinetmakers often clung to fading English fashions, but Virginia's leading artisans and their patrons were sensitive to London's dictates.

Thomas Chippendale knew, as well as any, that furniture is a decorative art and to succeed it must be beautiful as well as functional. The great eighteenth-century English master based his designs on tested classical proportions, and he urged his followers to study various ancient orders of capitals until they knew every line, each curve, the subtlest proportion.

Thus the apparent simplicity was deceptive. Moreover, the Williamsburg cabinetmaker was capable of the most exquisite, complex ornamentation when the job demanded it. The Anthony Hay shop — rebuilt and thriving today on its original foundations — produced ornate china tables of the best American type, adorned

A router cuts neat grooves in a piece of mahogany.

with blind fretwork, serpentine sides, vine and flower designs, a skirt of rococo cut-through carving, and tapered square legs ending in tassel feet. Some ornamental features associated with the Hay shop, like lion head arm terminals and dolphin feet, appeared nowhere else in North America.

Devotion to structural integrity marked all the known Williamsburg cabinetmakers. While New England furniture was built on the weaker patterns of English provincial furniture, Virginians relied on the stronger sophisticated structures of the advanced London type. Backs were paneled, full-bottom dustboards separated drawers, feet were built up in strong, shockproof composites, and dovetails were hidden.

Fine woods abounded in eighteenth-century Virginia forests. Walnut, cherry, maple, and pine were preferred among native woods. Once mahogany became available, the craftsman realized that its warm, rosy glow was perfectly suited for furniture and that it also resisted warping.

In urban shops, skills might be divided. Lathe turners, joiners, upholsterers, gilders, and carvers plied their specialties, and the master often functioned as a coordinator of skilled artisans as well as a salesman and decorator. Most shops, however, still required hands who could do it all.

Williamsburg masters preferred to hire skilled journeymen rather than employ indentured servants. The apprenticeship system also served as a source of labor. New trainees were instructed in four basic areas. Stock preparation was primary since nothing could be accomplished until the wood was straight and ready. After

aging outside for years, it needed attention. Joinery, or the mastery of dovetailing, mortising, and edge-joining, had to be so automatic that pauses for thought did not interrupt the work. Turning, carving, and the cutting of molding came next. The lathe was the most common power tool. It could be run by a handcranked flywheel, a treadle, or a waterwheel. The final training was in the application of finishes, which required a knowledge of chemical darkeners, vegetable dyes, artists' oil colors, shellac and oil varnishes, and waxes.

No cabinetmaker spurned producing modest furniture for the less grand, and they also installed complex drapery beds and made coffins. Undertaking was an integral part of the cabinetmaking trade in the eighteenth century. Instead of simple pine boxes, coffins were cloth-covered, velvet-lined, brass-nailed creations which were taken to their final destination in a hearse that the cabinetmaker provided as well.

Today the authentic Anthony Hay shop is a place where beauty glows from fine wood, classical curves, and honest structure — the qualities of furniture, Virginia-style.

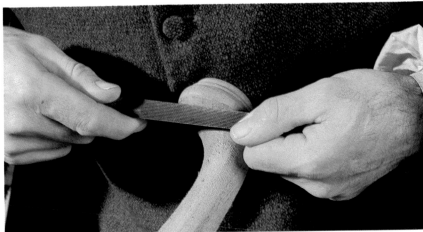

Williamsburg cabinetmakers were capable of highly ornate work, but Virginians preferred simpler — although highly sophisticated — shapes, like this pad foot.

Silversmith

The colonial silversmith was a merchant in grace and utility, importing from England tableware, cutlery, jewelry, buttons, shoe buckles, rings, and brooches. Watches and clocks ticked and glittered in his showroom, and if he sold them, he repaired them, too. If the smith was worthy of his name, he was also a sculptor, hammering loveliness from a precious metal for the privileged few.

When today's silversmith obtains an order for a new coffeepot, he fires up his forge and melts some silver in a graphite crucible, pouring the molten metal at 1,900 degrees into a cast-iron mold greased with tallow. The resulting ingot, a flat, nearly circular hunk of sterling (92.5 percent silver, 7.5 percent copper), is then hammered out into a flat sheet. The silver is pounded from the edges as the craftsman gradually stretches the ingot out, a process that work hardens the silver. To counteract the tendency toward brittleness, the smith returns the silver often to the forge, heats it to around 1,000 degrees, and quenches it in an acid bath called pickle. The process anneals the silver, reducing stress and making the metal flexible.

When he has a sheet of the correct thickness (whatever he wants the pot's walls to be) the craftsman pencils in with his compass a large

Hammers and anvils in various shapes and sizes are the basic tools of silversmithing.

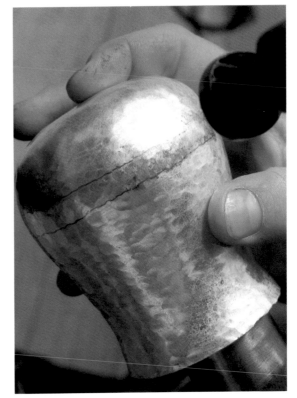

Lengthy hammering hardens the silver and makes it brittle, so the smith must heat the metal to 1,000 degrees to soften it, then quench it in acid or pickle, which cleans it. Then he begins hammering the small tankard again.

21

The scalloped design is filed into the edge of the tray.

circle, one he calculates will contain enough metal to make the central urn. Then he shears off the edges. Again wielding his compass, he draws a series of concentric circles from the center of the big silver wafer.

Starting in the middle, where the tiny mark made by his compass will always be the true center of the pot, the smith places the silver sheet on a finely polished anvil and begins hammering the silver down against the anvil with an equally smooth hammer. Around and around, circle after circle, he hammers. The silver begins to move, forming first a shallow saucer, then a bowl, then a gradually rising inverted parabola.

As the noisy transformation occurs, the silversmith changes his anvils, or stakes, according to the subtle demands of the pot's emerging baluster shape. He continues to refresh the penciled circles that must be followed lest the shape

Before it is soldered, the body of a beaker is wired together.

22

Raising the heat with his blowpipe, the silversmith melts soft silver solder into seams and joints.

swell in a lopsided bulge. Most of the work is in the left, or holding, hand; it is the sensitive positioning of the work on the stake that counts. The hammer blows are uniform and constant; keeping the metal at just the right angle is the controlling variable. "Shape it as you raise it" is the ancient rule of the silversmith. In the process, he returns the pot to the forge perhaps twenty or twenty-five times for annealing. Then, satisfied at last by the shape, he hammers lightly over the entire vessel twice again in the final smoothing process called planishing, a careful two-stage rapping to remove all hammer marks.

Making the basic body is a two-day job, but there is a lot more to do before the dull, vase-like object becomes a coffeepot. Base, finial, and spout halves are cast, a hinge is constructed, a graceful handle is carved from dense, smooth fruitwood. Then comes the painstaking process of soldering it all together. The smith does some soldering over the forge, but for fine work he employs a blowpipe method to heat his chips of fluxed silver and brass solder. He graduates downward the melting points of his various solderings so that the first steps are not remelted by the later.

Finally, after perhaps one hundred hours of work culminating in a final flourish of polishing with pumice, rottenstone, and jeweler's rouge, the shining coffeepot, an object both decorative and useful, is finished.

The faint hint of waviness on their rounded surfaces identifies these vessels as hand-hammered silver.

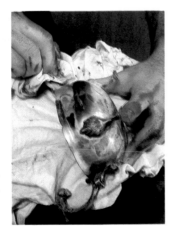

A final polish with jeweler's rouge puts a beautiful finish on an heirloom of the future.

The finished coffeepot is an elegant example of the art of the silversmith.

Engraver

Like that of the painter or sculptor, an engraver's equipment is simple. The skill lies not in elaborate procedures, or constructions, or the mastery of many tools and materials, but in some mysterious, ineffable connection between eye, brain, and hand.

The engraver contemplates a clear, shining surface such as a silver beaker on which the customer has commanded a monogram in script. The craftsman rubs his forehead and massages his nose. A nervous habit? Not at all. What he wants is light oil. With his fingers he smears it carefully on the beaker's surface and then dusts the area with talcum powder to produce a thin white film.

He reaches for one of the oddest tools in any craftsman's kit — a rose thorn, which is glued to the end of a pencil-sized stick. With the thorn's delicate point he must free-hand the monogram onto the powdered surface. From long experience he knows precisely how each letter must look; he does not need to glance at a book of characters to determine how each elegant swirl, each classic serif, must go. But the interlocking combination may cause some aesthetic problems of spacing and proportion. Dissatisfied, he repowders the surface and starts again. This time he gets it right; the loops are balanced, passing over and under one another like the tendrils of a vine.

The first cutting is done with a delicately pointed scriber as he traces the monogram's light outline. Now he can wipe away the powder and pick up his basic tool, a script graver. Like all his gravers, it is a simple, ancient device that has a blade with a wedge-shaped point and a bulbous wooden handle with one flat side. Palming the handle, pivoting his right thumb on his left index finger, the engraver starts the tiny wedge-shaped point on its first smooth bite into the silver.

As he deftly cuts out the smooth, curling lines, a process taking perhaps fifteen minutes, he turns the beaker as much as he changes direction with the graver. Propping the beaker on a leather sandbag makes it easier. Some articles do better supported by a sand-filled leather doughnut, and for small work such as rings and bracelets he employs a pitch pot that rotates in a doughnut-shaped leather bag. There are no other tools but a few gravers with points shaped for specialized cuts — block letters, flat bottoms, shading lines, and dots. There is one more tool that even the best workman must use now and then. It is a handle with a smooth steel curl affixed to it that is used as an eraser when he must burnish out a slip.

Occasionally an eighteenth-century Virginia engraver might have done the copperplate for printing currency or for a wealthy planter's bookplate. But usually he created the same things that people still want today from the rare practitioner of this authentic craft — graceful inscriptions that identify the proud owner of some object of beauty and value.

Tracing in the outline of a monogram with a steel scriber, the master produces a pattern that will be engraved later.

Following the scribed pattern, the master uses a steel graver to cut away the sterling and produce the desired monogram.

Boot and Shoemaker

The gulf between then and now seems wider when an unexpected difference is encountered, for example, that the colonial Virginian had two left feet. Or two right feet. It was all in the way it was viewed, for both shoes of a pair were identical.

There has been no anatomical change; the eighteenth-century Williamsburger was built like his modern counterpart. His demand for symmetry was so strong, however, that it was offended by lopsided footwear made for right and left feet specifically, and he wanted both shoes exactly alike. Every morning, to assure each would wear identically, he reversed their order of the previous day. The buckles then worn on all dress shoes did have a right and left direction, so he had to remember to rotate them daily as well. Occasionally, someone would demand shoes made explicitly for right and left, and the shoemaker would oblige.

Even if such a nuisance was endurable in the name of fashion, was it not uncomfortable? No, say those who try straight-on shoes today; they somehow feel just as comfortable as any modern shoe. So much for the need for right and left. And why should not such shoes be comfortable? They were made by a skillful craftsman, using the finest top grain leather.

An array of materials awaited the customer's pleasure, including — for the finest shoes and gloves — dog, a skin of great softness and beauty. Hence "putting on the dog" still means the ultimate in dressing up. The usual leathers were the ones still desirable today: steerhide for soles and heels (the latter built up with wooden pegs); calf for the uppers; linings of sheepskin or pigskin.

The vamp, or toe, section is one of the three main parts of an upper; the others are the two rear quarters.

After stitching the vamp and rear quarters together, the upper is soaked in water, then stretched and nailed to the last, a wooden form simulating the human foot.

For most of the eighteenth century, shoes were far more popular than boots. Men's shoes were usually black. Women and children had a wider choice of colors, and often the uppers of women's shoes were made of fabric.

The vocabulary of the eighteenth-century shoemaker sounds partially familiar. The essential wooden pattern for each size and style is called the last. The front or toe section of the upper shoe, the vamp, is first tacked tightly over the last. Then the welt is sewed to the vamp as the tacks are simultaneously removed, and the two rear quarters are joined to the vamp with ingeniously butted seams that are therefore smooth and comfortable. The insole, buttressed by a leather or metal shank beneath, is installed, and the sole is stitched on with flax by a technique called double running.

Most of the work occurs on a cutting board in the craftsman's lap. A bucket of water is nearby for the frequent soaking needed to make leather pliable. His "third hand," a wooden vise called a stitching clam, is never far away. His collection of tools includes an array of odd-shaped blades called roundknives, clickerknives, headknives, and lipknives. There are pricking wheels, channel tools, crimping boards, lasting pliers, and last pullers. He wields pegging awls, stitching awls, and scratch awls. Rasps, hammers, and templates lie close at hand.

On good days, he can turn out as many as two pairs of shoes. If demand for footwear is slack, he may produce some pitch-lined leather jacks, which may be used as beer and ale mugs. Or he may create a leather dice cup, or the frame of a hornbook, the paddle-shaped device that helped children learn to read. The shoemaker may also take in some repair work, although he does not think of himself as a cobbler, a term that in colonial days denoted an itinerant repairman of substantially lower skill and status.

The leatherworker uses a half-moon knife to shape the heel.

The sole is stitched through a hidden channel cut in the bottom as the craftsman holds the shoe down with a special belt called the stirrup.

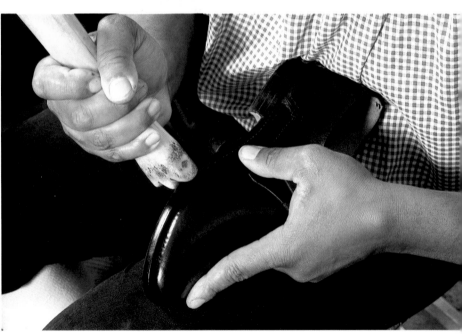

A burnisher made from animal bone smooths and polishes the edges of the sole.

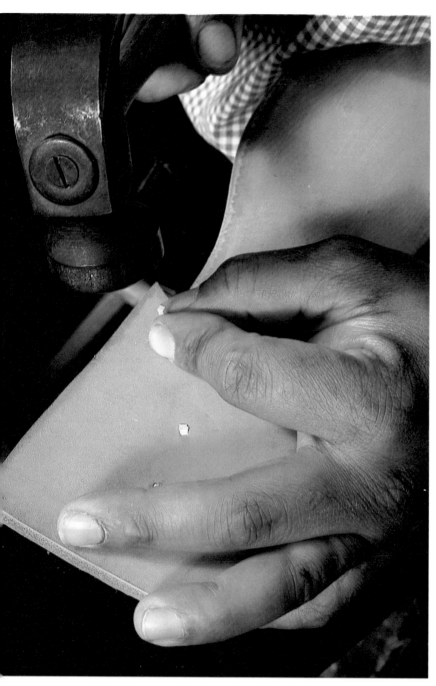

The shoepeg, a hardwood nail, is ideal
for holding layered heels together.

A pair of handmade shoes
awaits its new owner. In the
eighteenth century, the customer obtained buckles
elsewhere, probably from the
silversmith or milliner, or re-
used old ones.

Saddle and Harnessmaker

Were eighteenth-century crafts to be rated on the basis of how pleasantly their respective shops smelled, none but the baker's would outrank the harnessmaker's. Freshly cured leather — stiff steerhide rolled up like rugs, supple white leather, its softness belying great strength, patterned pigskin and furry deerskin — exudes an ineffable bouquet.

That the finished product smells so good is ironical, for the process by which leather is tanned is one of legendary stench. Tanyard, even today, remains almost synonymous with an operation that civilized communities banish to the farthest downwind limit. Objectionable but necessary, tanning hides is a complex and diversified process, depending on the breed of animal and the result desired, and it produces a wide variety of leathers of very different qualities.

In the eighteenth century, leather ranked with iron and wood as one of the most useful natural materials. There were leather water buckets, bottles, fire hoses, inkwells, and helmets, to mention just a few obsolete products in addition to the many uses of leather common today as then. There might be some overlapping with the local bootmaker, but generally the colonial Virginia

the stitching clam, a four-foot-long wooden pincer, acts as the leatherworker's third hand and allows him to exert the considerable strength his trade demands.

Saddles, harness, shot pouches, saddlebags, portmanteaus, and fire buckets were some of the items produced by an eighteenth-century harnessmaker.

saddle and harnessmaker concentrated on those two namesake staples of his trade, along with producing military accoutrements for the local militia. He handled other miscellany according to demand and time.

Steerhide was his chief raw material. In some applications it was a stiff, impregnable, full quarter-inch thick; in others, more tractable. Making a saddle required several gauges of hide. Saddlery, probably the greatest test of a leather-craftsman's skill, was also a creative challenge. There were hunt saddles, plantation saddles, hussar saddles, and sidesaddles, and most were custom made. Not only did the craftsman and the purchaser need to agree on the style and level of ornamentation, but each saddle, from its very foundation, the tree, was built to suit the dimensions of its future owner.

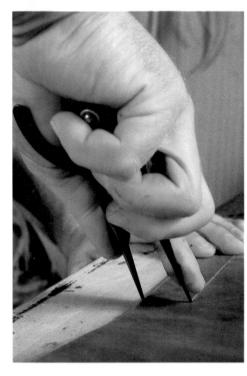

The harnessmaker marks off a steerhide strap.

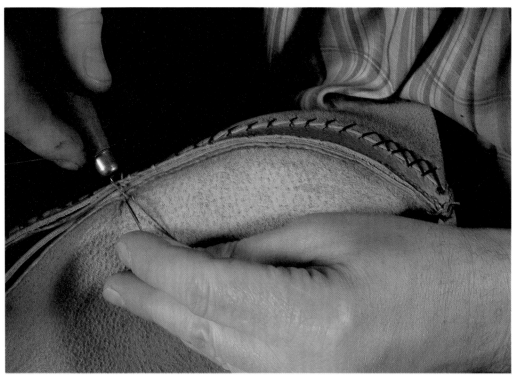

After piercing holes with an awl, the craftsman draws two opposing needles back and forth to produce the tough saddle stitch.

Much of the craftsman's work seems quite simple. He cuts long strips of leather and stitches them together, with appropriate mountings of hardware to make harness. The skill comes in choosing the right leather, cutting it quickly and perfectly, and stitching with strength and neatness. Tools are few, their origins lost in antiquity. The leatherworker's indispensable aid is the half-moon knife, whose rounded edge was commonplace as long ago as 1550 B.C. Wielded in conjunction with the stone (a foot-square chunk of polished granite mounted on a stump), the knife, at a flat angle across the stone, peels away slices of tough steerhide with buttery smoothness.

Neat stitching begins with the pricking wheel, whose point-studded roller marks a track of dots into the leather. Then, with a stitching awl, the craftsman pierces holes through the hide. His favorite stitching material is flax cord. Usually he wields two needles, passing them back and forth at the same time in a criss-cross or saddle stitch.

In the horsedrawn society of eighteenth-century Virginia, saddles and harness were much in demand, as were other impedimenta of the traveler. The portmanteau, a duffelbag-shaped case for clothing that was strapped behind the saddle, was a popular item, as were game bags and shot pouches for hunters.

One of the craftsman's more unusual specialties was a mundane domestic object, the colonial equivalent of the modern fire extinguisher. Traditionally made of leather, two-gallon buckets filled with water or sand hung in most buildings, ready to be used if an emergency occurred.

Built on a "tree" tailored to the customer's body, a custom-made saddle is expected to fit a horse and rider in complete comfort.

Blacksmith

In the eighteenth century, the blacksmith provided essential supplies and services to the public and to other craftsmen. Metal tires for the wheelwright, nails for the carpenter, and hoops for the cooper's barrels came from the blacksmith's shop, as did other objects needed by the coachmaker, miller, founder, silversmith, and shipwright, to name some of the other artisans who depended on the smith. The blacksmith also made and mended such items as tools, locks, and household articles in addition to shoeing horses. Clearly, everyone in Williamsburg patronized the blacksmith.

The forge, or fire, is an important feature in today's shop, just as it was two hundred years ago. The forge consists of a small raised brick hearth with a bellows to blow the fire and a hood above to carry smoke and fumes away. The fire itself is of bituminous coal; clinkers are carefully scraped out from below the hearth. The blacksmith soon learns how to regulate the intensity of the fire so that it produces the proper heat for the task at hand.

The smith does much of his work on his anvil, which has had the same basic shape since ancient times. It is made of wrought iron and steel that rests on a hardwood base and may weigh up to three or four hundred pounds. Hammers of various shapes and weights are used to work the hot metal on the anvil. Because iron transmits

Tongs are used to extract a variety of hot metal objects from the forge and hold them as the smith hammers.

The hammerman's deft strokes transform a bar of iron into a graceful curl.

The striker helps the smith to shape larger or heavier objects.

With a set of hammers of one to twelve pounds, his anvil, and anvil tools, the smith can make almost anything of iron.

heat readily, the smith employs a variety of different tongs to do the holding. Vises are used to hold articles during finishing operations, which may include bending, riveting, filing, and polishing.

Iron can be worked within a wide range of heat, but for many jobs it is heated to a temperature of about 2,400 degrees and comes out of the forge a bright yellow color. Different temperatures are best for different processes, however, and the smith must learn to control the forge and the hammer in order to obtain the optimum result.

Steel, which is worked at slightly lower temperatures, is needed for cutting edges, although it is not used for the entire product because of its high cost and toughness in forging. Controlled heating and quenching hardens and tempers the steel, resulting in either very hard or very tough articles such as axes, springs, hammers, files, and drills.

Welding is an ancient process by which two pieces of metal are joined together. Iron may be welded to steel; welding iron to iron or steel to steel is also common. Heating both pieces to about 2,400 degrees makes fusion possible, with the help of the hammer. The joint must be free of any scale or contamination if it is to be secure, so fluxing the weld to prevent oxidation is critical. Common fluxes include sand, borax, borax and wood ashes, or borax and iron filings.

Control of the hammer, control of the forging processes, and control of the fire — such are the skills that enable the blacksmith to produce items of lasting usefulness.

Filing and polishing change the character of iron objects and are often performed on household utensils.

Although most nails were made by professional nailers in the eighteenth century, some were occasionally made by smiths.

Hoes, hinges, firedogs, toasters, and bootscrapers are some of the blacksmith's useful contributions to daily life. 37

Founder

Sometime in the dawn of civilization man learned to smelt metals from ore and then discovered that some of them worked better when mixed together. Copper and zinc made brass; copper and tin made bronze. Founders learned such alloys' stubborn secrets through centuries of trial and error. By late medieval times, a technique known as sand casting was brought to high proficiency and the art remained unchanged until the twentieth century.

The eighteenth-century foundryman spent much of his time making products for other craftsmen. Some of the items that he created included brass castings for the gunsmith and cabinetmaker, silver handles and finials for the silversmith, and buckles for the shoemaker.

The hard part of foundry work today is not so much in melting metal as it is in making the fragile cavities that will receive it. The process begins with a master pattern of whatever is to be

Casting begins with making a master pattern. Atop the master, the foundryman tamps sand into an iron frame called a flask.

The mold must be prepared carefully.

Cutting gates in the sand will allow the molten metal to flow properly while gas escapes through tiny vents.

Shown are the two halves of a mold for brass candlestick bobeches.

produced. The pattern, which may be of wood, brass, or even plaster, lies in its own perfect bed in the master mold. The trick is to create a cavity matching the pattern's every detail. The foundryman packs ocher colored sand shaken from a sieve into an iron frame called a flask, set down on a duplicate that holds the master mold and the patterns of a candlestick base. The sand is velvety and cool; called "French casting sand," it contains enough clay to retain moisture and assure the impression of every fine detail. The mold-maker tamps the sand with a light, limber handled hickory mallet. Then he gently breaks the two flasks apart. In the fresh sand is the perfect hollow image of one-half the candlestick base. He repeats the process to capture the other side of the pattern. Both halves complete, he must carve out gates and sprues for the molten brass to run through when it enters a hole at one end of the completed mold. He cuts tiny vents through which gas may escape. The process, more complicated than this brief account would indicate, includes a number of other steps: the dusting of talc and red soapstone, the blowing of water mist through a copper atomizer, even scorching the final sand contour with a smoky torch.

Merged together, the two iron flasks now contain the perfect outline of the candlestick base. The new mold is placed on a stack of others, forming a column of ironbound molds about four feet high, and the entire group is bolted together and turned on its side with the sprue holes of each mold facing up.

Meantime the founder has been heating his brass to a molten state in a forge fire of coal. An apprentice tugs at a ceiling-mounted bellows to push air through a hidden flue into the firebox. In the heart of the fire, a tall clay pot glows orange; with iron tongs the craftsman lifts the lid. A blue green flame flickers forth. The founder knows from its color that the white-hot lava needs a touch of zinc and a pinch of borax flux.

Now comes the part demanding strength and nerve. The founder must pluck the crucible from the fire with tongs and pour the searing 1,900-degree mixture into the waiting sprue holes of six or seven molds. Smoke fills the shop.

Broken from its mold, the new candlestick base must be sawed from its stalk-like sprue and polished. The candlestick's tall central stem — like almost all cylindrical objects — will be cast in hollow halves and soldered together. Otherwise the process is the same, and, once used, each mold is broken up and the sand is reprocessed. Leftover brass is simply tossed back in the crucible.

Silver, gold, and bronze are cast like brass. The founder of nonferrous metals rarely pours iron, but he may ladle out pewter, the useful combination of tin, lead, copper, and a little antimony that was a household favorite for centuries. With a much lower melting point (only 600 degrees), pewter is poured into permanent bronze molds, a far easier system.

The final step is sooting the mold.

Brass is heated to about 1,900 degrees in a clay or graphite pot called a crucible.

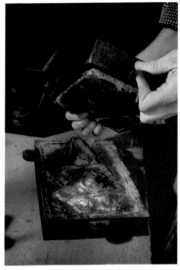

Lifting the crucible from the forge with tongs and tipping it to pour the molten metal into a small hole demands strong arms and steady nerves.

Carefully breaking the mold apart, the foundry-man reveals a candlestick base.

Nearly all cylindrical parts are cast in halves, which must be soldered together. After applying small pieces of solder and flux, the founder wires the halves together and heats the whole over his forge.

Grinding and polishing by file, lathe, and hand still remain to be done. Such tedious work is traditionally performed by apprentices.

41

Cooper

The craftsman one-handedly flips a four-foot white oak stave from end to end and glances down its curving flanks. He flips it back again, spying an errant bulge. Wielding his massive broad ax with casual grace, he flicks away a single oak sliver. Satisfied, he tosses the stave onto the growing pile.

Anything made of staves held together by hoops fell under the general classification of coopering, and there was clear specialization in the eighteenth century. White coopering encompassed products like buckets, churns, tubs, and dippers, which were often made of easily worked cedar or pine. The slack cooper made large barrels for non-liquid commodities like tobacco or flour, one-way containers that he turned out at the rate of ten per day. The trade's aristocrat was the tight cooper, whose white oak barrels would carry the world's precious liquids on continuous journeys for as long as thirty years. An experienced journeyman, working quickly, could produce two per day.

In this day of fork lifts, pallets, power winches, and truck-size containers, the barrel is nearly

The cooper shapes a stave at the large upside-down wood plane called a jointer.

43

Drawknives help the craftsman achieve the curves that will form a circle when the staves become a barrel.

ignored by all but vintners and distillers. But it was a perfect container for a pre-mechanized age. Not only was it strong and tight, it rolled. And properly it should be called a cask, for in the eighteenth century a barrel was merely one of a number of tight casks including the firkin, kilderkin, hogshead, butt, rundlet, tierce, puncheon, pipe, and tun.

White oak, the preferred wood, is dense, clear, nonporous, and predictable. From the center wood of a straight, perfect tree the cooper splits out rough staves. Splitting is easier than sawing, and the staves thus made are stronger because their grain runs parallel.

Then with his short-handled broad ax he gives each stave its basic bevel and taper, further refining the critical step with a jointer, a large, stationary wood plane with the cutting edge up. Sometimes the cooper uses a drawknife. Staves complete, he organizes them into a circle and secures one end of the fledgling barrel with a hoop called a gathering ring. The staves now are like petals on a closing blossom. The cooper heats the ensemble over a small stove to make the wood pliant.

Staves secured at one end by the iron gathering ring, the cooper begins driving down hickory trussing rings prior to slipping on permanent iron rings.

44

Coopering and its tools were passed from one generation of workmen to the next.

Ramming down a series of heavy hickory hoops called trussing rings, he begins forcing the staves together in a tight circle as the barrel takes form. Soon iron hoops made by a blacksmith replace the trussing rings. With a router plane called a croze he cuts inside grooves where the flat barrel heads will fit tightly in each end. The heads are a potential trouble spot and the cooper takes great care with them.

"A circle has no weak point" he says, and the barrel head is the only place there is the possibility of a leak. So like everything else, it must be perfect. How does he know when it's perfect? "You just have the feel. You *know*," the cooper laughs. As if that explains it all.

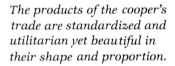

White oak staves were heated over a small stove called a cresset until they became pliant enough to be easily bent.

The products of the cooper's trade are standardized and utilitarian yet beautiful in their shape and proportion.

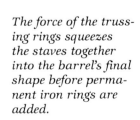

The force of the trussing rings squeezes the staves together into the barrel's final shape before permanent iron rings are added.

45

Musical Instrument Maker

The eighteenth century was a time of great interest in music, a time when many people played one instrument or another. Expertly or wretchedly, with most of them probably somewhere in between, Virginians bowed violins, plucked guitars, or blew on recorders, while the vibrant, full tone of harpsichords made in England and imported to the colony sounded in well-appointed homes.

Most instruments came from Europe, products of such factory-like shops as Jacob Kirckman's of London, specialist in harpsichords. A skillful musical instrument maker may have found opportunities in the colonies. Williamsburg cabinetmaker Benjamin Bucktrout, for example, advertised in the *Virginia Gazette* in 1767 that he could make and repair harpsichords and spinets.

Each piece of spruce or maple that goes into an instrument comes from a tree that grew in a particular spot containing its own unique mixture of minerals. A clever apprentice thus needs years of experience before he can consistently recognize the latent acoustical qualities in a piece of wood.

The craftsman selects spruce, which is strong for its weight and tonally excellent, for the soundboards of stringed instruments. The backs of violins are always made of maple because it can be shaved thin enough to vibrate well and yet remain strong enough to support string tension.

Based on the wood he chooses, the maker decides how to shape the arches of the instrument he is creating. If he wants a light, fluty sound, he may need to fashion a high arch, especially if the

The musical instrument maker knows exactly how much wood to remove from a violin's soundboard to obtain the most tone from the wood.

Scraping, not sanding, is the preferred method of removing wood from a violin's maple back.

Carving the scroll at the end of the maple neck is an artistic touch that precedes gluing the violin's fingerboard.

47

Tiny cutting thumb planes, some as small as a fingernail, are used to shave the spruce soundboard of a violin.

spruce is soft, because the higher the arch, the lighter the sound. In a soundboard of hard spruce, a low arch may produce a violin of powerful, brilliant sound. Yet he must also skillfully counterbalance the spruce front with the maple back.

The musical instrument maker sensitively scrapes, bends, and glues the fragile appearing elements. At one point, he actually tunes the nearly completed top and back with the aid of a bow and a tuning fork. Carving the scroll, gluing the ebony or boxwood fingerboard, inletting delicate lines of reinforcing strips called purfling — all must be done with the final complex relationship in mind. Then, complete at last, the violin is coated with a slow drying oil-based varnish, a process that may take four months, and with twenty coats of varnish, finally rubbed with rottenstone to a brilliant shine.

With its expressive tone and tractable volume, the violin was truly the queen of eighteenth-century instruments. Already perfected as the century began, it led the way through an era of changing musical fashion. Other instruments, like the lute and the viola da gamba, fell from favor. Guitars, however, remained popular throughout the century.

Thin strips that will become the walls of a guitar are dry-bent around a bending iron, a small stove that contains an alcohol lamp.

A guitar of eighteenth-century style and tone will take shape inside this wooden mold.

The mastery of tiny saws is essential for the musical instrument maker who attempts the difficult skill of marquetry.

This four-inch boxwood lute rose has been saw pierced and carved.

The guitar of the eighteenth century was more delicate than its twentieth-century counterpart.

Elaborate inlay on the neck of a lute.

Still life in the musical instrument maker's window — violin, cittern, and viola da gamba.

49

Wheelwright

In eighteenth-century Virginia, the wheelwright and his associate, the coachmaker, tailored their work to demands that were more utilitarian than stylish. There was a heavy demand for two-wheeled carts and for a handy, tough, lightweight two-wheeler for personal transportation called the riding chair, or simply chair. There was also a constant need for wheelbarrows. Thus colonial Virginia was a good market for wheels.

The hub begins as an elm, locust, or birch tree from which a section of foot-thick trunk is aged at least seven years. The hub is shaped on a lathe to precise contours and then is bored with a special tapered reamer. Into the hole goes the wheel's bearing surface, a hollow cone of bronze, iron, or brass called the box, which the wheelwright has ordered from a foundry.

Much basic geometry goes into the building of a wheel. The craftsman draws concentric circles (usually on his shop floor) depicting each shape and dimension. The complement of spokes, usually twelve or fourteen, is determined by the wheel's outer portion, the ring. A perfect wooden circle is formed of arcs called felloes, mortised together. The spokes, spanning hub and ring, are also mortised into place. Spokes of ash, hickory, or white oak are best.

The wheel now looks complete, but despite the craftsman's careful joinery it would soon fall apart on the road without a final element, its tire. Fitting the iron rim begins with a precise measurement of the wheel's circumference, followed by a quick order to the blacksmith, who makes the tire to seamless perfection. Placing the tire flat

The hardwood hub turns under the wheelwright's gouge.

Long aging of the right wood, usually elm, birch, or locust, helps to assure a sturdy, long-lasting hub.

on the ground, the wheelwright builds a circle of fire over it, bringing the iron to a temperature just short of red-hot.

Wielding long-handled tongs, the master and a helper carefully drop the hot iron onto its waiting wheel. The tire has expanded about one inch in diameter, and now it shrinks quickly as the craftsman douses the wheel with water. A few smart raps from the wheelwright's hammer and the new wheel cools into a tight, rugged whole. Later the wheel will be painted, then slipped onto the tapered iron axle spindle of a cart and fastened with a linchpin, just in time to take to the road.

The spokes are mortised into the wheel's curved wooden outer ring, which is made of a series of arcs called felloes.

The master shaves a spoke while his helpers saw a felloe from a hardwood blank.

52

A hot iron tire that has expanded about one inch in diameter is lowered onto the wheel, tapped into place, and cooled with buckets of water.

The completed wheel should roll trouble-free for thousands of miles.

Building Trades

Styles may change, but carpentry endures. Saw, chisel, mallet, scribe, hammer, and nail: they have altered little through the centuries.

Thus erecting a house in eighteenth-century Virginia was similar to building the same structure today. The time required for building then was not much greater than now, if construction hours only are counted and not those required to shape and prepare all the building materials. The systems whereby trees became beams, boards, and shingles; clay fire-hardened into brick; and iron forged into nails were simpler but slower than today's comparable processes.

Boards and beams, for example, were often produced by hand with a two-man rip or pit saw. With the log mounted over a saw pit dug into the ground, one sawyer (the pitman) stood underneath while the other stationed himself on top of the log. The two men worked the huge saw down the length of the log, tracking a line made by snapping a taut chalk or charcoal covered string. Some water powered sawmills existed, but where they were too far away, the pit sawyers prevailed.

Hand-hewn beams were used extensively because large construction beams were beyond the

Although sawmills existed in eighteenth-century Virginia, the use of the saw pit was commonplace. Before cutting, the sawyers mark each log with a chalkline.

Wedges keep the two-man saw from binding as the sawyers produce beams and boards.

55

capacity of early sawmills. So even where mills were nearby, such beams were hewn out with the broad ax. The hoe-shaped adz, although occasionally used as a timber finishing tool, was more often employed to thin and shape the surfaces of boards.

House framing techniques in eighteenth-century Virginia were poised somewhere between the Middle Ages and the present day. One practice was cutting joints to connect the timbers, a stronger but more involved method because it required chiseling of mortises and tenons, than the modern nailed fastening. The colonial builder, however, did use nails in great numbers in weatherboarding, floors, and roofs.

Eighteenth-century carpenters made greater use of planes than do their modern counterparts. There were more rough surfaces to smooth, and molding was shaped on the site.

Frame timbers are prepared on the ground by carpenters, who cut mortises and tenons and then mark each timber for assembly.

Carpenters made their joints on the ground and numbered each timber prior to erecting the frame so that they could be sure the fit was right. Timber dimensions were not so capricious as one might think; a member measuring three by four inches was the two by four of its day.

Much of the carpenter's skill lay in knowing the various strengths and weaknesses of the woods he employed. Oak, locust, and tulip poplar were often used, while hard yellow pine was the mainstay then as now. Shingles made from select pieces of cypress, juniper, oak, chestnut, or heart pine were split first with a tool called a froe and then sometimes shaved with a two-handled drawknife. Floorboards required mature and resinous heart pine and also had to be quarter sawn, or cut so that their exposed surfaces were at right angles to the growth rings of the wood. Moldings, windows, and doors were also of pine, their components having been shaped with the aid of special planes.

Rose-headed nails, forged by local blacksmiths, are standard fasteners for weatherboards and flooring.

Hardwood pegs lock framing together securely.

Colonial construction techniques involve much shaping by hand.

57

When there was no large project to work on the craftsman stayed busy with tasks like repairs and alterations on homes and barns. There was an endless demand for fences.

At a major construction project, the man in charge could be the master carpenter or the master mason. Either had to act precisely as to-day's contractor does, organizing, coordinating, and making sure all the workers were busy because they were hired by the day. Construction in eighteenth-century Virginia was largely a capitalistic venture with little of the spirit of communal assistance that became a cliché of frontier epics.

The shinglemaker's tools include the hatchet, froe, mallet, and drawknife.

Shingles are made of cypress, juniper (white cedar), oak, chestnut, or heart pine.

Clay is the sole ingredient of Virginia bricks.

Mixed with water, the clay is stirred until it becomes a thick mud.

Bricks for a big structure with masonry walls and several chimneys were sometimes made on the site. Virginia's subsoil is usually an accommodating mixture of clay with enough sand to make good bricks. Few manufacturing processes are as convenient to set up as a Virginia brickyard.

Clay is dug, mixed with water to make uniformly stiff mud, slapped into wooden molds, removed, and dried in the sun. Animals may track across their damp surfaces, and worms may crawl through, drilling neat holes. The drying takes around five days, during which the brickmaker prays for dry weather because rain will erode and ruin his bricks, of which he has probably made twenty thousand or more.

The brickmaker's real skill begins with stacking air-dried bricks into their kiln. Still highly vulnerable to rain, the bricks are arranged in elaborate, interwoven heaps crisscrossed around

The brickmaker, standing in a barrel-lined hole, takes mud as it squeezes from the mill and slaps it into wooden molds.

A single wet brick weighs about eight pounds; dry, it will weigh five.

connecting tunnels. Fire tunnels, or eyes, penetrate the entire stack at ground level. At last, his house-sized kiln completed and sealed over with mud, the craftsman starts his fires.

A huge column of smoke and steam begins to rise above the kiln, signaling the emergence of moisture and impurities. It will last at least twenty-four hours. Then the air clears as clean heat waves shimmer over the kiln for five more days. Stoking the eyes, the brickmaker raises the heat to 2,200 degrees. He looks for a red glow at the top of the kiln, followed by stabbing fingers of fire, that tell him the clay is changing to brick at last. He raises the heat even more, to 2,500 degrees, and waits for a tell-tale slump, a slight swayback, to appear in the roof. It is time to stop firing and seal the openings.

The mass will gradually cool for up to two weeks before workmen can start dismantling the kiln. Its outermost bricks never get hard enough, and are tossed aside for use as fill. Next come fairly soft, salmon colored bricks, destined for interior walls. Perhaps half the kiln will produce well-baked bricks, the best of which are found above the fire tunnels. They are decorative, glazed-end bricks, created by heat and potash in the fiery chemistry of clay and hardwood.

Sun drying on the ground may take as few as three days or more than a week, but usually about five days. Drying bricks are vulnerable to assorted natural hazards.

The kiln is an elaborately stacked mass of bricks that is sealed with a coat of mud. Fire tunnels, or eyes, penetrate the kiln.

Miller

Post windmills were spreading across Europe by the twelfth century, and for six hundred years afterward they hardly changed. The one owned by William Robertson, a citizen of means in Williamsburg in the eighteenth century, was much like its prototype of several centuries earlier.

The windmill is a tall, narrow, two-story house mounted on a massive central oaken post, braced in turn by four quarter bars. Its construction enables the mill to rotate and face the wind instantly whenever it changes. Such is the ingenious construction of a post windmill that one man can turn it easily.

Four twenty-six-foot sail frames are mounted on the wind shaft. Attending to the sails — knowing how and when to reef the linen sail cloth to the wind and keep it tight — is critical. The blade angle is fixed, and each frame is weighted for balance at the end. The mill requires at least a 10 mph wind, but from 20 to 30 is preferred, blowing as steadily as possible.

As the sails turn, the mighty wind shaft rotates in tallow-greased bearings at the top of the mill house. Just inside the upper chamber, like a wheel on an axle, a great gear called the rack, bristling with fifty-one wooden teeth, transmits the horizontal motion of the shaft into vertical rotation through a wooden cage gear called the pinion. Beneath the pinion lies the heart of the windmill, the two round granite millstones. The pinion's iron shaft is mounted in the top, or running stone, which grinds atop the fixed bed stone. A hexagonal wooden hopper, built above and around the running stone, funnels grain into the grinders. In the room below, fresh meal sluices down a trough, runs through a quaking sifter to discard the chaff, and pours into a waiting sack.

Even by modern standards it is a complex procedure that is governed by the capriciousness of the wind. The miller must tell by sound and feel if all is well. There is a throbbing, a bump-

ing, a slight rocking from side to side when the mill is running properly. With no tachometer to guide him, the miller must simply know by experience when his running stone (carefully leveled, and balanced with lead) is at the correct 105 or 110 revolutions per minute, or five times around for every revolution of the sails. To control the speed, he tugs a rope that clamps a giant wooden brake shoe on the rack wheel. But that is just one constantly monitored adjustment. The amount of grain going to the stones must be exactly right, a measurement bound not only to the speed of the grindstones but by their spacing as well. For the running stone cannot just drag heavily around on the bed stone; it must be delicately adjusted for the proper gap. The miller sets the measurement by working a long, throttle-like lever called the lighterstaff.

In colonial days a mill could grind as much as two hundred pounds of cornmeal per hour. It was and still is hard work, and sometimes dangerous. Such mills were the scenes of dreadful accidents. Moreover, the miller was often maligned — sometimes with reason — for being of less than total probity. He might adulterate his flour with sawdust, or give dishonest weight, or, through assorted tricks, hold back more than the one-sixth toll that was his due from each customer's grain. Virginia passed strict laws to control such deception, and if Mr. Robertson's miller got by with much, he was clever indeed. But let us be charitable and assume that he was both successful and honest.

Dangerous as well as ingenious, the pinion (left) is driven by the fifty-one-tooth rack gear mounted to the main shaft. Power is thus transmitted to the running stone.

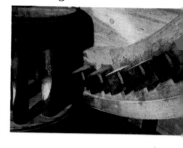

Grain is hoisted to the upper floor of the mill. It goes from the bin at the left into a hole above the running stone, shown here by the miller's right hand.

Baker

Bread was indispensable in eighteenth-century Williamsburg. Producing the staff of life was physically taxing, and the baker's trade was a hard one. Up by 3 a.m. to start his fires, stooped from carrying bags of flour and huge wads of dough, often working in oppressive heat, the baker toiled to produce Williamsburg's daily bread. In addition to bread, he offered an assortment of other confections such as tarts, cakes, deep-dish fruit pies, puddings, and custards. Game and poultry pies were other favorites from the baker. Although kitchen sanitation requirements were minimal, his products tasted good and probably would suit modern palates better than some other colonial cookery.

White flour was preferred for bread. The imperfect bleaching and bolting techniques of the time, however, resulted in an off-white product that had a far richer taste than today's powder-fine version. To make bread the baker mixed sugar or honey with milk and melted butter and scalded the mixture with boiling water. He added yeast and then stirred in flour. When the mixture grew bouncy he kneaded it, then put it away in the coffin-shaped dough box for about two hours before forming his hand-shaped loaves, which rose for another hour and a half.

Meanwhile, the baker prepared the oven. A standard oven of the day for a commercial establishment was a brick igloo about four feet in diameter and one and one-half feet high. Of prehistoric origin, such dome ovens are found in many cultures. There was no flue inside; instead, the oven was vented through its open iron door into a hood. The oven was fired with a blaze of hardwood sticks for about two hours, then the embers were scattered around the oven floor to spread the heat, after which they were raked out.

Hot bricks, not fire itself, did the baking. When firing, the heat inside might reach 600 degrees, but the baker — testing the heat by thrusting his arm inside — waited for a 350-400 degree oven to start baking. Small, quickly baked items like biscuits went in first; heavy pastries, which needed deep baking, came last.

In eighteenth-century Virginia, breads and pastries made from wheat flour were preferred by those who could afford them; ashcakes, hoecakes, and corn pone were also popular.

The baker can tell from the look and feel of the dough when he has kneaded it long enough.

Wigmaker

Mankind's inordinate emphasis on a fashionable appearance culminated in the eighteenth century, the golden age of wigs. Louis XIII of France popularized wig wearing in the 1600s when he began sporting a huge wig of brown ringlets, a style later favored by Charles II of England and other royal heads. The greater the personage, the more magnificent the wig — hence the faintly derisive term "bigwig" entered our common parlance.

As frontier conditions in the Virginia colony gave way to the greater polish of the eighteenth century, the fad crossed the Atlantic and took root in towns like Williamsburg. Few colonial ladies wore wigs, so although some shops accepted female trade, most Virginia women retained their own hair and dressed it themselves.

There was still a vestige of the barber's ancient bloody heritage — the supposedly beneficial practice of bleeding, from which the barber pole evolved. A short pole festooned with spiraled bloody rags and crowned with a bleeding basin was the original inspiration for the still familiar tonsorial symbol, and there is some evidence of bleeding and tooth extraction by Williamsburg's barbers and perukemakers.

But mostly the trade was all for fashion. The Virginia gentlemen yielded to no London fop in demanding wigs in a variety of styles. The powdered wig was for formal occasions; for everyday use a man chose whatever color he liked, the most popular being brown, black, blond, grizzle, or mixed black and white.

An inveterate wig wearer would have his own wig block, carved to his precise head measurements and usually stored at his favorite wigmaker's. A properly fitting wig had to fit the skull perfectly and since there was no elastic in those days, it required a complicated foundation of ribbons, netting, and silk fabric called the caul.

The hair to be attached to the caul was imported from London dealers and had originated on the heads of impoverished peasant girls. Horse and angora goat hair were also used occasionally. The strands arrived loose, as well as often dirty and greasy; the craftsman first cleaned and degreased the hair with mill dust or sand, then combed it through a steel-toothed brush called a hackle. Permanent curls, if desired, were created by wrapping the hair on ceramic or wooden rollers, boiling it in water, and baking it in an oven.

The hair was then woven together on a small bench fixture called a tressing loom that produced fringes called wefts. One after another, the wefts were built up on the caul until the wig was made. The wig's final styling was determined during this process. To fix the styling, the craftsman added pomade — boiled, scented lard.

A regularly shaved head was essential to wig wearing; neglecting to shave the skull might produce the embarrassing phenomenon known as flipping one's wig. Still another wig-age expression endures today. Formal wigs powdered with flour mixed with cornstarch required repowdering as a night of revelry progressed. Thus the well-ordered home or tavern designated a small room, or closet, for touching up. It was, of course, the powder room.

Taking several strands of hair by the root ends, the wigmaker weaves them on the silk threads of a tressing loom to create fringes called wefts.

Milliner

Milan was Christendom's fashion center in the Middle Ages, and one who peddled the desirable goods from that Italian city was called, accurately or not, a Milaner. Thus "milaner" may have metamorphosed into milliner. Or milliner may have derived from "mille," the Latin for thousand, since eighteenth-century milliners offered a profusion of goods for sale.

By the eighteenth century, the milliner's shop had become virtually a small department store. A well-stocked establishment might contain jewelry (necklaces, earrings, lockets, watches, brooches), fabrics (damask, silk, satin, brocade, dimity, flannel, osnaburg, nankeen, bombazeen, cambrick, demi-cambrick, huckaback, pullicat, and harrateen), shoes, buckles, muffs, fans, combs, stationery, purses, soap, dentifrice, snuff, hoops, clamps, and clasps. Sometimes a dress-maker worked on the premises.

But whatever the eighteenth-century milliner stocked, she always offered hats, since the wearing of headgear by men and women alike was very fashionable in the 1700s. Men's hats

and some women's hats and caps were made in Europe and imported to the colonies; many ladies' hats, however, were created by the local milliner. A Virginia milliner, conscious of the changing dictates of London fashions, was limited only by her imagination in producing the extravagant confections demanded by her clientele.

Starting with a screenlike segment of sized buckram, she steam-shaped it over a block for the basic foundation, sewed the brim to the crown, and then added linings, feathers, or other embellishments. Ostrich feathers, curled and dyed, cock feathers, pheasant feathers, dyed duck feathers, even swan and guinea feathers decorated eighteenth-century hats.

There were also assorted odd specialties like the calash, a huge cloth covering for the high, exaggerated hair styles worn by some fashionable women. Finally, because many men wore wigs, requiring shaved pates, the milliner supplied nightcaps that were so necessary to keep bald heads warm at night.

A stiff white fabric called buckram is steamed over a wooden block to give proper shape and size to the hat.

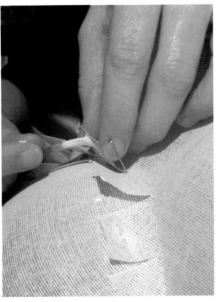

The brim of the hat is sewed to the crown.

Narrow picot ribbon is sewed into the brim to act as a hatband. It helps to retain the shape and also covers the inside seam.

69

Domestic Crafts

Domestic work in the Virginia colony — was it a craft, minor skill, or simple drudgery? Probably it was a mixture of all three. Clearly most such work was the province of women and slaves, an accepted social imperative of the time.

Textiles

All things considered, producing fabric was the most complex of these homely activities. Most Virginians' fabrics were imported from England, but a few households — chiefly large plantations — were self-sufficient enough to produce some of their own cloth.

Linen was a leading fiber until the rise of King Cotton around 1800. Once words such as scutch, break, line, retting, and tow were commonplace, but the vocabulary of flaxbreaking vanished with the disappearance of the noisy, simple device that did the job, a wooden crusher called the flax break. It shattered the carefully retted and dried stalks of flax, separating fiber and crushing pith. The mess was then combed, or hackled, to produce strands of line, now known as linen. Its coarse, short fibers, pale yellow and soft, were called tow and were used to make towsacks, while the seeds, removed in a process called rippling, became linseed oil.

At their gently humming wheels, patient women spun the fine strands of line (or wool or cotton) into thread. Spinning is actually twisting. The fibers are first wound lightly on the teardrop-shaped distaff. Then the spinner's fingers form a stream of fibers that are simultaneously pulled and twisted through a racing axis called the flyer and onto the bobbin. The spinner must know exactly how much fiber to feed to the flyer.

A coarse comb called a hackle removes pitch from the crushed flax and frees strands of line, or linen.

Dried flax stalks are crushed in one of the initial steps in making linen.

For domestic workers of the eighteenth century, drudgery such as carding wool was lessened by making it a social occasion.

71

Once spun, the yarn might be bleached or dyed. The dying of yarns and fabrics, especially wool, was commonplace in rural households and may have been done in Williamsburg, although commercial dying was also available in town. Walnut hulls for brown, indigo for blue, and apple bark for yellow were all handy. Imported madder and cochineal for reds were stocked in Williamsburg stores and apothecary shops. Such dyes were mixed in hot water in which the wool or other fiber was dipped long enough to achieve the desired color. Metallic salts were added to set the dyes.

After it was dyed the yarn was ready to be woven into cloth on the loom, a complex arrangement of beams, strings, and rollers, with a comb-like sley mounted in the beater to

Guided by the operator's skilled fingers, strands of linen supplied from a loose gathering on the distaff are spun or twisted into thread on the spinning wheel.

After carding and spinning, wool was nearly always dyed. Vegetable dyes were commonly used.

72

monitor the distribution of thread. Much of the weaver's skill — apart from knowing how to prepare the complicated loom itself — lies in handling the shuttle. The shuttle holds a bobbin of thread that must journey horizontally (the woof) alternating with the vertical (or warp) strings. After each toss of the shuttle, the weaver pushes up the beater to tighten the threads in their fixed pattern. Fine homespun fabric is the product of the weaver's loom.

Four-harness looms produced homespun fabrics in attractive patterns.

73

Getting the wicks to dangle straight is more difficult than it looks.

Few could afford the luxury of candle molds although they made better looking candles.

Candlemaking

Candles provided the main source of artificial light in eighteenth-century households. Beeswax, bayberry, and tallow were the usual raw materials for candlemaking; dipping and molding the usual techniques. Sweet smelling bayberry was pleasant to use and free for the taking in the lowlands near tidewater Virginia beaches, although a single candle required the waxy essence of fourteen quarts of the small berries. Dipping was faster and cheaper (there was no need for an expensive mold), but the candles made by even a skilled dipper were never smooth, perfect tapers like those from a mold. A careless dipper's work resembled parsnips more than candles.

Wax for dipping was heated to about 180 degrees in a copper kettle. Wicks of braided cotton, wool, or flax twist dangled from the hand-held racks. After a dip or two the wicks

started curling up on the bottom end and each had to be straightened. Bayberry candles needed forty-five dips, beeswax only thirty.

The process was easier for those sufficiently well off to own candle molds. After the wicks were pulled through the long cavities and tightened on skewers, molten wax heated to 230 degrees was poured from a spouted pot. Drying took about four hours. A dash of cold water on the outside of tin molds loosened the candles quickly, while hot water worked better on pewter ones.

Basketmaking

Light, strong containers of infinite shapes and uses, baskets were indispensable in the eighteenth century.

White oak is the favored material, although ash, hickory, cedar, reeds, and willows also make good baskets. Picking the right tree is a knack learned only through long experience. Clear, perfect, straight grain is desired. Although it is a wood noted for its hardness, white oak comes apart easily in the hands of a skilled basketmaker.

The craftsman begins with a six-foot section of trunk perhaps ten inches in diameter, splitting it into halves and then quarters. He removes the reddish heartwood to save for hoops and handles and continues splitting until the original tree is in one-sixteenths. So far, he has used wedges and an ax. Now he wields the only other tool a basketmaker needs, a large pocket knife. Starting at each telltale growth ring on the end of the six-foot split section, he peels away strip after strip with ease.

Stripping must be done within eight weeks after the tree is cut, while it remains fully green. Once stripped, the long white ribbons of flexible wood are woven into square, round, or oblong baskets without further treatment. Or the weaver may form the bottom of a chair, first selecting the desired pattern — plait, wicker weave, or twill. Most of the basketmaker's projects will take about four hours and will serve for years.

1.

2.

3.

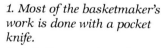

The basketmaker begins by selecting a live tree, which he fells and brings to his shop. Baskets may be made of many woods, but the favorite is white oak, tough, supple, and surprisingly tractable.

4.

1. Most of the basketmaker's work is done with a pocket knife.

2.-3. Before starting a basket, the craftsman calculates all the specifications of material, shape, and weave that will produce the desired container.

4. Beautiful in their useful simplicity, handmade baskets may last almost indefinitely.

Food Preparation

Meals had to be prepared daily in every colonial household, and in a large, well-ordered one cooking was a full-time job. Since there were no stoves, the kitchen fireplace was the center of culinary activity. Coals, not flames, were the preferred source of heat; iron and copper vessels were hung from above or supported by trivets from below over the hot coals. Sometimes an oven was built into the chimney for baking breads, cakes, and pies.

Curing and smoking pork occupied about six wintertime weeks in most households. Hams, sides, and shoulders were steeped in salt, rolled in pepper and molasses, and smoked over a hickory fire, while sausages, head cheese, and lard were prepared from pork byproducts. Bristles for brushes were useful inedibles.

A vegetable garden and perhaps a few fruit trees were carefully tended on nearly every property. Horses, cows, pigs, chickens, and even a few sheep — all might have been found in eighteenth-century Williamsburg, and most were under the supervision of the busy housewife.

Laundering

Laundry work was not performed in every household; there were laundresses in town who handled wash for some families. Soaps of various types were available in Williamsburg shops, but some rural households made their own. Lye, leached from fireplace ashes, was boiled for hours with fat or lard to produce a hard gray green soap. Common fabrics were boiled in soapy water until they came clean. White bread crumbs rubbed into the soiled area removed grease spots. Starch was made from potatoes, and indigo produced bluing. Flatirons, heated on coals, did the pressing.

Domestic crafts may not have demanded the training or the polished performance of commercial trades produced by the apprentice system. Yet many an eighteenth-century homemaker or servant was a model of versatility who moved quickly and competently from one domestic activity to another in a lifetime of long hours, taking pride in the management of a well-ordered household.